D0549363

Roman Britain

By
Gillian Osband
Illustrations by
David Simonds

Contents

Kingfisher

The Story So Far

When the Romans started their invasion of Britain in 55 BC, they were in the process of conquering Gaul (France). There were rumours that Britain was a rich country with productive metal mines – and as the Roman general Julius Caesar was just across the Channel it must have seemed an ideal moment to come and have a look. At that time, the people of Britain were mostly busy with farming and metal crafts, although they had some trade with other countries.

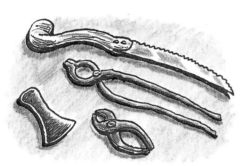

Britain was inhabited by Celtic tribes living in different small kingdoms spread over the country.

Many lived in homesteads, often on hills and defended by ditches and ramparts to form hill-forts.

Their houses were round huts made of wood or stone. They did not have drains, sewers or running water.

Some southern tribes were skilled in metal work. But in the north, stone and flint tools were still used.

The tribes sometimes fought each other, but they had no proper army. Each tribe had its own tactics and rules.

Travelling could be a risky business. There were no proper roads, just muddy and winding trackways.

In 55 BC the Romans were highly organized and were ruled by a single powerful government.

The Romans built many cities throughout their empire, with stone buildings, sewers and plumbing.

They had schools, hospitals, a complex legal system, literature and poetry, philosophy and art.

They had communal bath houses with hot water and even a form of hot-air central heating.

Their army was highly trained, disciplined and well-equipped. Roman soldiers were real professionals.

They built roads that were strong and usually straight, to let the army and other people travel easily.

The Mighty Roman Army

The spread of the Roman Empire was partly due to the fact that the Roman army was so well organized. It was divided in two groups – legionaries and auxiliaries. Every soldier knew his role and there was a clear chain of command. The army was well-trained and well-equipped, and also highly disciplined. It was a winning combination, and there was no other army like it.

Commander in Chief

The legion commander, or legatus legionis, was from a wealthy Roman family.

Legendary Legions

Legionaries had to have been born Roman citizens and served in the army for 20 years. When they retired they would receive a pension. About 6000 men served in a legion, including about 120 horsemen. Every legion had a name and number, and a silver eagle – the symbol of the Roman Empire – as its standard. If the standard was captured, it was a terrible disgrace.

The Chain of Command

The foot soldiers were divided into groups of 100, called centuries. Each was led by one of 60 centurions. Six centuries would be joined to make a cohort, a unit of about 600 soldiers. The legion was made up of ten cohorts, giving a total of 6000 soldiers. The commander of the legion was helped by six officers, called military tribunes, who were often at the start of a political career.

Auxiliaries

Auxiliaries were recruited from conquered lands. They were paid less than the legionaries and had to serve for 25 years, after which they became Roman citizens. They were led by Roman officers, in infantry cohorts, of 500 or 1000, and smaller cavalry groups called 'alae'. Auxiliaries were armed with bows, darts, slings and dolabras – a cross between a pick and an axe.

Army Life

Soldiers living in forts trained hard, with a route march of about 30 kilometres each week and drill once or twice a day. They had instruction in swimming and stone slinging, and had to be able to vault onto a horse – there were no stirrups in those days.

Life was even harder for soldiers on the move. At the end of a day's march they had to build a camp. Each soldier carried a pack with spare clothes, food rations, a cooking pot, a short spade, a handmill for grinding corn and two wooden stakes to help build a protective fence.

Make Your Own Roman Armour

With a bit of planning you can kit yourself out like a Roman soldier. Here are some suggestions.

Make your cassis from a colander covered with foil and stick on cardboard cheek-pieces. Wear a long brown T-shirt and a scarf for your cingulum and focale. Wear dark leggings or track-suit trousers rolled up a bit for your brachaei. Wear ordinary sandals for caliga and make your gladius, lorrica segmentata and other armour from painted cardboard. A wide leather belt across your chest gives you somewhere to keep your gladius between battles.

Roman Armour

Every legionary wore the same basic armour.
1. Cassis – a metal helmet with leather cheek-pieces.
2. Lorrica segmentata – armour of metal strips.
3. Focale and cingulum – scarf and tunic worn under armour.
4. Leather apron with protective metal discs.
5. Brachaei – leather breeches.
6. Caliga – heavy leather sandals with studded soles.
7. Pilum – a javelin about 210 centimetres long.
8. Gladius – two-edged sword about 60 centimetres long.
9. Curved shield made of layered wood and leather.

A legionary's armour had to strike a balance between being light and easy to move in, and protecting him from enemy arrows and spears. Just as well you won't be facing any fierce tribes in this home-made version.

Cut out strips of cardboard, paint them to look like metal and sew them together using a darning needle and string, to make the segments of body armour.

Use a broom handle and cardboard blade for a javelin.

Make your breastplate and a similar piece to protect your back with cardboard. Punch holes in the sides and tie the front to the back with string.

Invasion

The Romans came to conquer Britain in two main campaigns, separated by almost 100 years. The first was led by Julius Caesar in 55 and 54 BC, the second by Aulus Plautius in AD 43. In-between, the Roman system of government changed from a republic, ruled by an elected group of people, to an empire ruled by a single emperor.

Caesar's Campaigns

Caesar's first raid was in 55 BC. He had just conquered Gaul (France) and there was a chance he would be called back. So when he set sail with his force of 10,000 men and 500 cavalry in 80 ships he knew he had to work fast.

The Britons had gathered near Dover, ready for battle. They were fierce fighters but the Romans won. The chiefs in Kent submitted and Caesar returned to Gaul.

A year later Caesar came back to Britain. This time he brought 25,000 legionaries and 2000 cavalry in 800 ships. They fought their way north of the Thames, where they faced an attack led by a tribal king called Cassivellaunus, who ruled the area around modern Hertfordshire.

Both sides wanted peace. Within two months the southern Britons had agreed to pay a yearly tribute of money to Rome, and Caesar left in triumph.

Roman Tactics

Although the Britons were fierce fighters, the Roman army overwhelmed them with its tactics.

The legionaries would throw their javelins, then rush in for close fighting with their swords. They held their shields close together to form a protective wall or roof as they advanced. Cavalry protected the legion's flanks, or sides, to stop them being surrounded.

For attacking towns and fortifications the Romans specialized in war machines – catapults, battering rams and towers.

The Next Stage

In AD 43 Emperor Claudius sent an army of about 40,000 to conquer southern Britain properly. The main battle took place near Rochester. After two days' fighting the Romans won the battle.

The commanding general, Plautius, waited for Claudius to arrive from Rome to lead the army to final victory. The emperor brought elephants with him to impress his new subjects.

The Great White Horse

In the Chiltern hills near Westbury there is a huge white horse cut into the chalk of the hillside. This is thought to be the symbol of the Catuvellaunian tribe. The horse shape was changed in the 18th century, but the earlier outline can just be seen from the air.

How to be a Roman Detective

If you visit a Roman site, look out for:
1. Carvings of the symbol of mighty Rome – an eagle, chosen because it was the king of birds.
2. Coins used by tribes in Britain between the two invasions. Some have the names of tribal kings written on them, others have pictures.

Forts and Walls

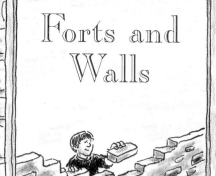

The Romans were well aware that some of the tribes in Britain did not accept their rule – there were sometimes uprisings led by tribal rulers in various parts of the country. So when the Romans conquered an area they would make it secure by building forts and fortifications.

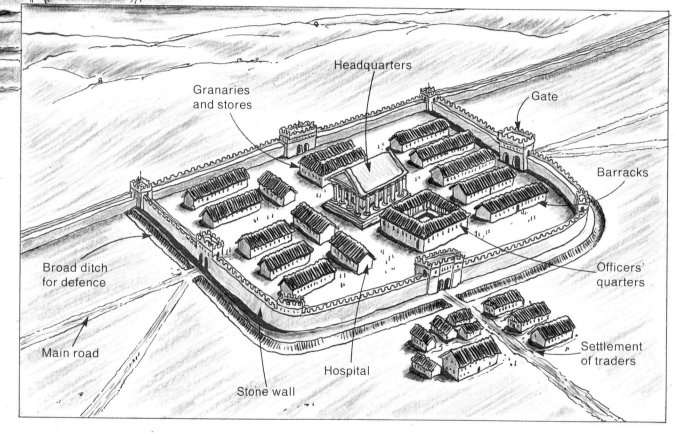

Headquarters

Granaries and stores

Gate

Barracks

Officers' quarters

Settlement of traders

Hospital

Stone wall

Broad ditch for defence

Main road

Roman Forts

There were three major forts in Britain, at Chester (known as Deva to the Romans), Caerleon-on-Usk (Isca Silurum) and York (Eburacum). There were many smaller forts at other important sites too.

They were all built to the same design: rectangular with four gates, and a main road leading in from each. The headquarters – the principia – was at the middle. It housed the standard for the legion, pay-chests and accounts. There were offices for the clerks and a great hall for ceremonies. In addition there were armouries, baths, cookhouses, a prison, a school for junior officers, and a military cemetery – gravestones were carved with a picture of the soldier and details about his life and career.

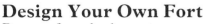

Design Your Own Fort

Roman forts had two important roles – they had to house a lot of people in reasonable comfort, and they had to act as a stronghold against rebel attack. As well as the buildings already mentioned, a fort would need a sewerage and drainage system and fresh water wells. Try and design the perfect Roman fort to house your own legion and defend it against attack.

Hadrian's Wall

The Romans managed to conquer Scotland but found it hard to keep under control. So they built a wall that stretched right across from Newcastle to Carlisle. The wall was planned in AD 122 by Emperor Hadrian and still bears his name. Later on, in about AD 140, another wall – the Antonine Wall – was built, further north. Both were eventually abandoned.

Hadrian's Wall was made of about 2 million tonnes of rock and soil. It was 116 kilometres long, 6.3 metres high and about 2 metres wide. There were 16 main forts along the wall, about 8 kilometres apart, each housing 1000 auxiliaries. Smaller 'milecastles' were built in-between, each with 50 auxiliaries, and between these were two watchtowers.

Building Towns

The Romans were used to living comfortably in their home towns and were certainly not prepared to be any less comfortable in Britain. The local tribespeople, who were used to living in wooden huts with earth floors, must have been fascinated by the huge, stone-built towns, with their running water and glass windows.

Planning a Town

The Romans left nothing to chance when building their towns. They had architects, surveyors, engineers and town planners.

Look at this reconstructed plan of Calleva Atrebatum (Silchester, near Reading). You can see the square street plan that was typical of Roman towns. Like forts, Roman towns had four gateways with roads leading to the centre. The towns were walled, at first with earth ramparts then later with stone.

In the centre was the forum – a group of buildings around a market square, with the town hall and law court along one side, and offices and shops along the other sides. As well as the forum, there were

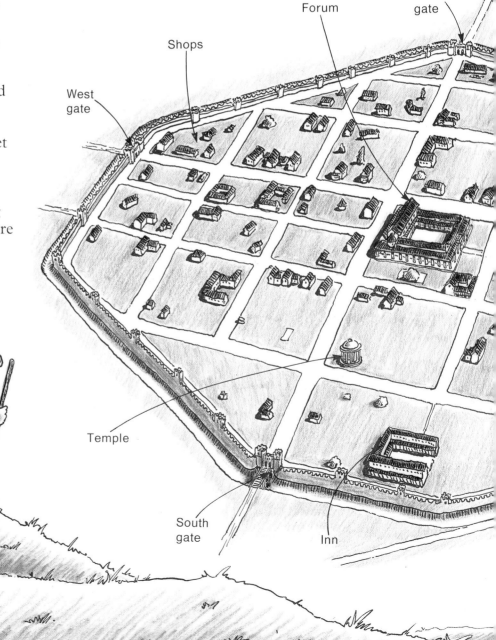

Shops

Forum

North gate

West gate

Temple

South gate

Inn

public baths, temples, shops, inns, barracks and houses. Just outside the town wall was the amphitheatre, where people came to watch sports and other displays that were regularly staged there.

New Ways of Building

Although Romans designed the towns, it was usually the conquered Britons who had to build them. They had to learn many new skills, such as how to make and decorate round stone columns; how to make slate or tile roofs that did not leak; and how to make sliding shutters. The Romans also introduced central heating with under-floor furnaces, and plumbing and drainage systems.

How to be a Roman Detective

Some Latin place-names are still used today, but they may be disguised. The Latin word for fort was 'castra'. Over the years it often changed to 'chester', 'caster' or 'cester'. Towns which were once Roman forts may show this by their names – Winchester, for example. The Romans called their paved roads 'strata', so places with names like Chester-le-Street or Stratford may also be Roman.

Civilization

Our word 'civilization' comes from the Latin 'civilis', meaning citizen. For the Romans, town-dwelling was the only civilized way to live.

Temple

Amphitheatre

East gate

Town wall

Large fosse or defensive ditch

Public baths

11

Roads and Travelling

Before the Romans came to Britain, travelling was slow and difficult. Footpaths and trackways followed winding courses, often along ridges or river valleys. The Roman idea of road-building was completely different – they knew the shortest distance between two points was a straight line and so they made their roads straight.

Strategic Routes

The Romans knew that good roads were needed to control a large empire. Troops and supplies often had to be moved quickly, and messages would have to be received with minimum delay. Road-building was, therefore, an essential part of the growth of the empire.

The Romans never did things by halves – their roads were built to last. We still use some of them today, more than 1500 years later. They are easy to recognize because they are so straight. Have a look at a modern road map and you should spot them easily – the Fosse Way, Watling Street and Ermine Street are three of the longest, but there are many others. Don't forget, they will often be linking towns that were important settlements in Roman times.

Some Roman Roads and Towns

- Hadrian's Wall
- Carlisle
- York
- Chester
- Lincoln
- Wroxeter
- Colchester
- Caistor
- Leicester
- Gloucester
- St Albans
- Caerleon
- London
- Cirencester
- Bath
- Exeter
- Canterbury
- Dorchester
- Silchester
- Ilchester
- Winchester

Building the Roads

The line the road would follow was marked out in advance. A foundation of large stones was laid on the soil with a layer of gravel on top to make a smooth surface. The road would be higher in the middle than at the sides so rain water could drain off into ditches. Paved roads were also built, with stone slabs laid on a base of sand and rubble.

Travel by Water

Roads were important for the army and government, but the waterways came into their own for transporting heavy loads – like grain, coal, or pottery. Roman engineers improved natural waterways and built canals, such as the Cambridgeshire and Lincolnshire Car Dykes. These also drained some of the low-lying areas, so that more land could be farmed.

Roman Milestones

To help travellers find their way, milestones were placed along the roads at distances of 1000 Roman paces (1480 metres). The Latin word 'mille' means 1000. The milestone would show the distance to the nearest town, the name of the ruling emperor, and even repair details.

Design a Milestone

Design your own milestone. Write in some useful facts for travellers – how far to the end of your road, when it was built, who was the king or queen at the time, the distance to the sweet shop, and so on.

Everyday Life I

Town life in Britain changed enormously under the influence of the Romans. Life was affected on every level you could think of. Here are just a few of the things you would have found if you had lived in Roman Britain.

Shopping

The Romans were great traders and because their empire was so large, they could import products from far-flung countries. Some tribes in southern Britain already traded with tribes from northern Gaul (France), but the Britons must have been amazed at the new products the Romans brought with them. There were shops in the forum where you could buy imported as well as locally produced food. The Romans had a taste for luxury, and there was demand for imported pottery, glass, bronzes, silverware, wine, oil, jewellery and cloth.

Money

Some tribes made their own coins, but soon everyone was using Roman currency. There were:
Asses – small bronze coins, smaller than 1p.
Sestertii – bronze coins about the size of 2p.
Denarii – silver mixed with copper, smaller than 5p.
For expensive purchases there was also the aureus, a small gold coin.

As

Sestertius

Denarius

Show-off Emperors

The emperors used the designs on the coins as a way of showing important events, both at home and abroad. They might show the emperor and his family, and portray some of his achievements. The designs on both sides were changed often – in one year the denarii was changed one hundred times and the sestertii over fifty times.

Keeping a Record

Merchants and traders needed to keep careful accounts of their business affairs. They used a kind of coarse paper with pens made of bronze or sometimes pointed reeds, and ink made of soot. Writing tablets were also used. These were made from two pieces of wood, hinged together. The inside was covered with a layer of wax. By pressing into the wax with the pointed end of a 'stylus', made of bone or metal, messages could be written. The stylus was flattened at its other end and was used to smooth the wax over to 'rub out' any mistakes that were made.

Make Your Own Writing Tablet

You need: a flat piece of wood about 15cm × 7cm, a small knitting needle, 2 wax candles, a foil dish, sheets of newspaper.

Ask an adult to turn the oven on to a low heat. Put the candles in the foil dish and put them in the oven to melt.

Check the candles every few minutes and once they have melted ask the adult to take the dish out.

Spread the newspaper out (to avoid making a mess). Put the wood in the middle and ask the adult to pour the wax gently over it until it is evenly covered.

Once the wax has set, you can use the pointed end of the knitting needle to write on it, and the rounded end to smooth over any mistakes.

Papyrus scrolls

Stylus

Roman wax tablets

Roman families who came to live in Britain brought many of their customs with them. Things like education, religion and law were very important to them, and some of their ideas are still in use today.

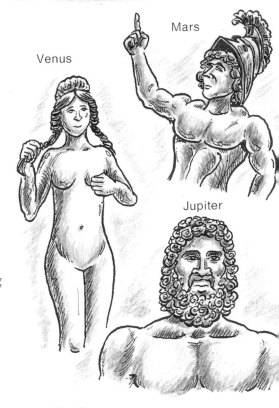

Venus

Mars

Jupiter

At School

Children started school, or were taught at home, from the age of seven. Lessons started early and ended in the afternoon. They learned to read, write and to do maths, and they used a stylus or paper and ink, and an abacus – a counting frame with rows of beads.

Children who went further with their schooling learned to speak Greek as well as Latin. They would learn about history, philosophy, literature, poetry, music and gymnastics.

Gods Galore

The Romans worshipped many gods and goddesses, like Jupiter – king of the gods, Mars – god of war, and Venus – goddess of love. After the reign of Tiberius, AD 14–37, emperors were worshipped too.

Roman and British religions blended and, as long as Britons honoured Roman gods, they were left in peace. But after AD 200, Christianity started to pose a threat to Roman rule. Christians would not even pretend to accept Roman gods.

Latin Puzzle

The language the Romans spoke was called Latin. Many Latin words are still a part of our language. Here are some English words and the Latin words they come from. See if you can pair them up.

Latin	English
Bracchium	People
Bellus	Round
Crudelis	Tavern
Humanus	School
Populus	Beautiful
Portus	Cruel
Rotundus	Human
Schola	Branch
Taberna	Port

Answers on page 24.

Roman Arithmetic

The Romans used a different method of recording numbers from the one we know. Here are the numerals the Romans used; they are still used sometimes today as well. Can you see how they used their numerals to make different numbers?

I	–	1	VIII	–	8
II	–	2	IX	–	9
III	–	3	X	–	10
IV	–	4	L	–	50
V	–	5	C	–	100
VI	–	6	D	–	500
VII	–	7	M	–	1000

See if you can work out what these figures are in ordinary numbers.

XXXII

CLIV

MDX

Answers on page 24.

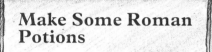

Make Some Roman Potions

To revive someone who has fainted.

You need: a small glass bottle with a cork, vinegar, fresh mint.

Pour some vinegar into the bottle until it is three-quarters full. Tear the mint leaves up and drop them into the bottle. Seal the bottle with the cork, shake and leave it for 24 hours. Remove the mint and store the bottle of vinegar in a cool place. When you need to revive someone, take out the stopper and hold the bottle under their nose for them to smell.

A poultice for chilblains.

You need: two or three turnips, a saucepan of water, a clean tea-cloth or hanky, newspaper.

Put the turnips in the saucepan of water. Ask an adult to cook them until they are soft – about 20 minutes – and drain them. Then mash them and let them cool down a little. Put the newspaper under your feet, spread the warm mash over your chilblains and wrap a clean hanky or tea-cloth over the top. Leave the poultice on for about an hour.

Life in a Roman Villa

In the southern half of Britain especially, wealthy landowners, merchants and tribal leaders built themselves large, stone 'villas' to live in.

Villa Living

A villa was a splendid type of farmhouse surrounded by its own land. Everything would be 'Roman' in style. Rooms were often rectangular. There might be a hypocaust (central heating) system and a suite of bathrooms.

The sites of about 500 villas have been found in Britain. You can visit some of them, and Chedworth in Gloucestershire is a very fine example. Here is a reconstructed plan of a typical villa.

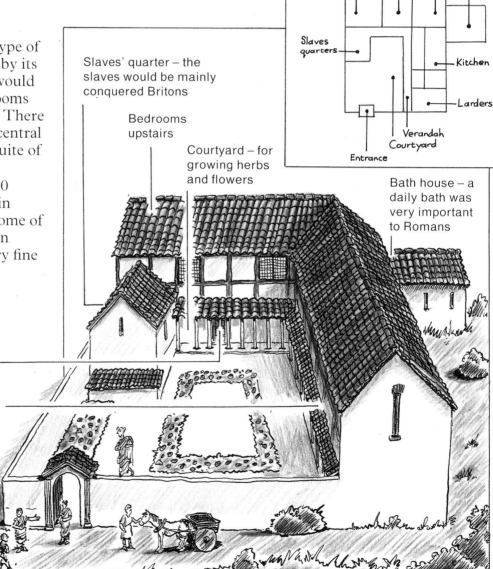

Summer room

Entrance hall

Heated room

Bath house

Slaves quarters

Kitchen

Larders

Entrance

Verandah
Courtyard

Slaves' quarter – the slaves would be mainly conquered Britons

Bedrooms upstairs

Courtyard – for growing herbs and flowers

Bath house – a daily bath was very important to Romans

Verandah – a Roman feature, less useful in a cold climate

Larders and stores – for produce from the villa's farmland

Keeping Warm

British weather must have been a shock to the Romans, but they had an answer for every problem. Building hypocausts into their villas kept them cosy. A hypocaust was an early form of central heating, which relied on hot air, heated up in a furnace, passing through channels in the floors and walls.

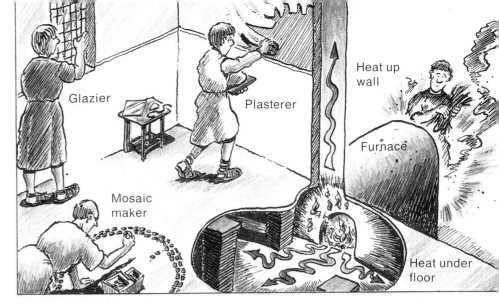

Glazier

Plasterer

Heat up wall

Furnace

Mosaic maker

Heat under floor

Decorating a Villa

The walls inside the villa were coated in fine plaster. Before it dried, a design was sometimes painted onto it so that the paint sank into the damp plaster.

The floors in the more important rooms were covered in mosaics – patterns and pictures made up of small coloured pieces of stone and brick, set into plaster while it was wet.

The Romans used glass windows, but after the Roman Empire collapsed the art of making them was forgotten and they did not reappear in Britain until the 13th century.

Make a Mosaic

You need: a large sheet of white paper, a pencil, scissors, paste or glue, pieces of coloured paper.

This mosaic was found in the Roman town of Pompeii, in Italy. The Latin words mean 'Beware of the dog'.

A Roman mosaic maker would spread plaster on the floor and press coloured stones into it. You can do it the easy way! Cut the coloured paper up into small pieces. Invent your own pattern, or copy the one shown here onto your paper. Spread glue on a small area and stick the paper shapes down, leaving a little gap between each one to look like plaster.

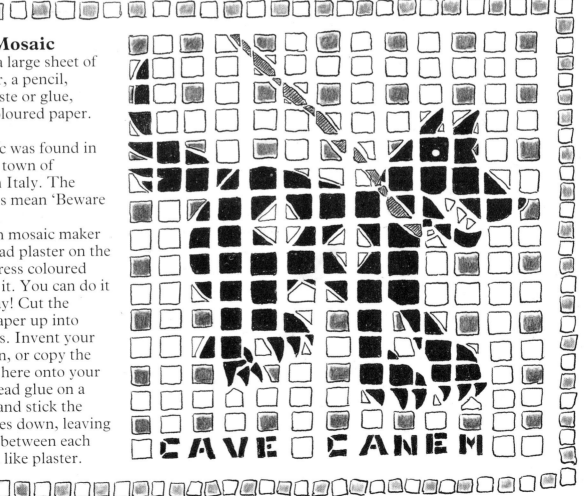

CAVE CANEM

19

My Day

My name is Juliana. I am XIII years old and a slave in the household of Marcus Agricola. It is autumn, in the third year of the reign of the Emperor Trajan.

Up early as usual. All the slaves have to be ready to look after the family from the moment they wake up.

6.30am

7.30am

Food! It's going to be a busy day as my master has important guests dining with him. I may not have time later so I'll fill up on milk, oatcakes and cheese while I've got the chance.

12.00am

9.00am

11.00am

My mistress's children have lessons in the morning. I try to listen to the lesson too while I sweep out the schoolroom.

I have been excused my other house-cleaning duties today so I can practise playing my harp for this evening's entertainment.

Starving! A quick dash into the kitchen to get something to eat. Everyone is bad-tempered as they are getting ready for dinner tonight.

My mistress and the other women are visiting the baths early today so my master can take his visitors there when they return from hunting. Phew! It's too hot for me, I can't wait to get out.

Now I have to start getting my mistress made-up and dressed. She's wearing some new jewellery that was brought from Rome only last month. I love that new perfume oil too.

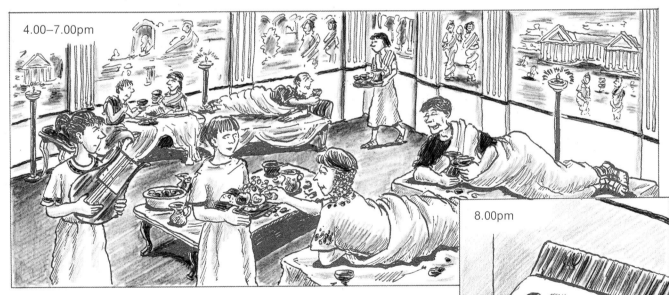

The special dish today is stuffed and roasted dormice – yum! We are using the best Samian ware so I must be careful not to break anything. If I trip over the leg of that couch again, like I did the last time, I'll just die of embarrassment.

Ten courses later – and they have all had too much wine. Nobody is listening to me play! Never mind – there are lots of leftovers in the kitchen! Then to bed. I'll be busy tomorrow, helping to set up the looms to weave cloth for winter cloaks.

Roman Romps

The Romans loved games and entertainment. Some of the things they enjoyed seem strange to us now, but others are more familiar.

A Visit to the Theatre

Pantomimes based on stories about the gods were popular. But theatres were also used for sports and games.

Games were held on public holidays. Wrestling, boxing, jumping and discus-throwing were common, but there were more blood-thirsty spectacles too, involving fights between animals, gladiators and animals, or even two gladiators – to the death!

A Roman Toy-Box

If you opened a toy-box in a Roman home, here are some of the things you would find: baby rattles; balls; dolls made of wood, bone or clay; pull-along horses and chariots made of clay; hoops and tops; darts; board games like draughts; glass counters; dice and knuckle bones.

Leap Frog, Hide and Seek, and Blind Man's Bluff were all games that children played in Roman Britain. All kinds of ball games were popular, with children and adults alike.

Trigon – a Roman Game

You need: 3 players and 3 balls.

The players form a triangle. Each has a ball. On the word 'Go' each player throws their ball to the right and catches the ball thrown from their left. Go as fast as possible without dropping the balls.

End of an Empire

Britain prospered under Roman rule for over 200 years. But by the 3rd century AD the political problems in Rome were weakening the empire's strength. Rebels and raiders took advantage of the situation by attacking the more remote parts and the Romans found they just couldn't fight them all off.

Attacked From All Sides

During the 4th century AD the Picts, unconquered tribesmen from beyond Hadrian's Wall, joined forces with Irish tribes in raiding the north of Roman Britain. In about AD 367, they and the Saxons – fierce Germanic pirates – attacked Britain and defeated the Roman army. Even villas in the south of Britain were looted by the invaders.

Reinforcements were sent by the Emperor Valentinian and peace was restored for a time. But the once-mighty empire was falling apart. Corrupt and greedy emperors and politicians weakened the army and not all of the barbarian raids carried out around the empire could be fought off. Things went from bad to worse.

Troops were gradually withdrawn from Britain to defend Rome itself. By AD 410, Emperor Honorius told the citizens of Britain they would have to defend themselves. Rome itself was sacked the same year.

Dressing Up Like a Roman

First of all you need a tunica – a long plain nightdress without sleeves would do. Tie a leather belt around your waist. Then you need a toga – an old white sheet is best. Fold it diagonally, hang it over your left shoulder and tuck the corner into your belt. Wrap the other end around your back, up under your right arm and over your left shoulder. Pin it in place with a brooch.

Places to Visit

- Aldborough, North Yorkshire – mosaic pavements, wall towers and museum.
- Ambleside Roman Fort (NT), Cumbria – gates, towers and granaries.
- Bath, Avon – Roman baths, public buildings based around the natural hot spring, mosaic floor, museum with many remains.
- Brean Down (NT), Somerset – remains of Roman temple and fields.
- Chedworth Villa (NT), Gloucestershire – mosaics, baths and a shrine.
- Chester, Cheshire – fortress remains, excavated amphitheatre, fortress wall and buildings, and a hypocaust.
- Dolaucothi (NT), Dyfed – gold mines.
- Hadrian's Wall (NT), Northumberland – milestones, Housesteads Fort.
- Letocetum (NT), Staffordshire – bath house and courtyard.
- London – London Wall, Museum of London and British Museum.
- Lullingstone, Kent – baths, wall-paintings, reconstructed mosaics, tannery and fascinating remains.
- St Albans, Hertfordshire – museum and remains from the Roman town Verulamium.

Answers

Page 16: Latin Puzzle

Bracchium – Branch
Bellus – Beautiful
Crudelis – Cruel
Humanus – Human
Populus – People
Portus – Port
Rotundus – Round
Schola – School
Taberna – Tavern

Page 17: Roman Numeral Quiz
XXXII – 32
CLIV – 154
MDX – 1510

KINGFISHER
An imprint of Larousse plc
Elsley House, 24-30 Great Titchfield Street,
London W1P 7AD
First published in 1989 by Kingfisher

20 19 18 17 16 15 14 13 12

BRITISH LIBRARY CATALOGUING IN PUBLICATION DATA
Osband, Gillian
   Roman Britain
   1. Great Britain, 43–410
   I. Title   II. Simonds, David
   III. Series
   936.1′04
ISBN 0 86272 422 8

Edited by Meg Sanders
Designed by Ben White
Cover design by David Jefferis
Phototypeset by Southern Positives and Negatives (SPAN), Lingfield, Surrey
Printed in Spain